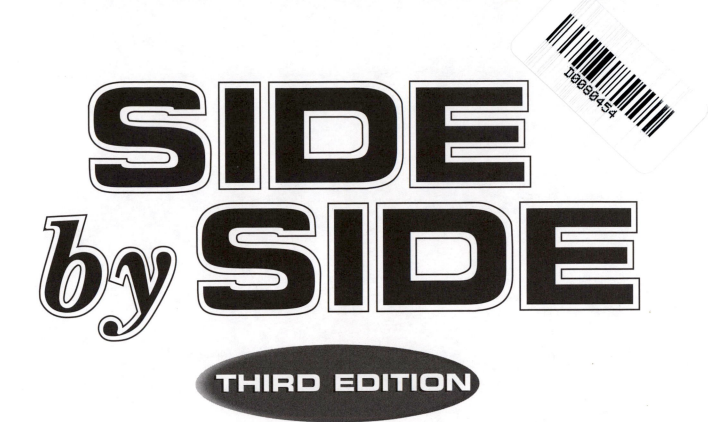

SIDE *by* SIDE

THIRD EDITION

Testing Program 4

Steven J. Molinsky
Bill Bliss

Contributing Author

Robert Doherty

longman.com

Side by Side Testing Program 4, 3rd edition

Pearson Education, 10 Bank Street, White Plains, NY 10606

Vice president, director of publishing: *Allen Ascher*
Editorial manager: *Pam Fishman*
Vice president, director of design and production: *Rhea Banker*
Associate director of electronic production: *Aliza Greenblatt*
Production manager: *Ray Keating*
Director of manufacturing: *Patrice Fraccio*
Associate digital layout manager: *Paula D. Williams*
Interior design: *Paula D. Williams*
Cover design: *Monika Popowitz*

Illustrator: *Richard E. Hill*

The authors gratefully acknowledge the contribution
of Tina Carver in the development of the original
Side by Side program.

ISBN 0-13-026890-9

1 2 3 4 5 6 7 8 9 10 – TCS – 06 05 04 03

Student's Name		I.D. Number	
Course	Teacher		Date

CHOOSE

Example:

Charlie _____ swum in a long time.

a. has
b. hasn't ⊛
c. didn't
d. doesn't

1. Andrew _____ songs for many years before he became famous.

a. had written
b. has written
c. has been writing
d. is writing

2. _____ Ms. Lee been playing golf for many years?

a. Is
b. Has
c. How long has
d. Was

3. Fran _____ to quit her job a few weeks ago.

a. has decided
b. had been deciding
c. decided
d. is deciding

4. Carol _____ becoming a pilot until she flew in an airplane.

a. hasn't considered
b. has to consider
c. had been
d. hadn't considered

5. Elizabeth _____ breaking up with Alan for a long time.

a. was
b. is thinking about
c. has been
d. has been thinking about

CHOOSE

Example:

Jason and his sister have been studying _____ this morning.

a. in
b. from
c. since ⊛
d. for

6. _____ has it been since we last met?

a. How long
b. When
c. How often
d. Where

7. Marie hasn't eaten lunch _____ today.

   a. already

   b. still

   c. yet

   d. recently

8. George didn't study for his history exam _____.

   a. last night

   b. in a long time

   c. since last night

   d. now

9. Has your cousin called you _____?

   a. at that time

   b. recently

   c. for a long time

   d. until this week

10. _____ the time Jerry arrived, we had already left.

   a. When

   b. From

   c. In

   d. By

CHOOSE

Example:

She's _____ that many orders before.

   a. been taking

  (b.) never taken

   c. taking

   d. ever taken

11. _____ practiced the piano for more than three hours?

   a. Have you never

   b. Did you ever

   c. Have you ever

   d. Did you never

12. Susan _____ very hard before she got fired.

   a. hadn't been working

   b. hasn't been working

   c. hasn't worked

   d. has worked

13. _____ since we met in college.

   a. We went out

   b. We've been going out

   c. We've already gone out

   d. We're going out

14. Mr. Brown _____ the kitchen when the phone rang.

   a. has been cleaning

   b. cleaned

   c. has cleaned

   d. was cleaning

15. Donald _____ inventory almost an hour ago.

   a. has taken

   b. took

   c. didn't take

   d. had taken

CHOOSE

Example:

I've _____ fed the dog this morning.

a. never

(b.) already

c. still

d. haven't

18. James wasn't paying attention _____ the teacher called on him.

a. because

b. since

c. then

d. when

16. Lawrence had driven to the bank _____.

a. this morning

b. in a while

c. the day before

d. since yesterday

19. Kathleen has been working at that restaurant _____ she was thirty.

a. for

b. since

c. when

d. while

17. My father had been working there _____ before he got laid off.

a. for many years

b. a long time ago

c. in many years

d. in a long time

20. Our children are _____ studying for their exams.

a. yet

b. still

c. ever

d. never

Student's Name _____ Date _____

WHICH WORD?

Carl | has had   (had)   had had | a terrible time last weekend on his camping trip.

He was upset because | had he   he was   he had |²¹ been planning it for a long time.

He had | been buying   bought   got |²² a new flashlight and a new pair of boots.

He had also gotten a new map, but he couldn't find it, so he | had   has had   had had |²³

to buy another one. Also, he | wasn't   is   had been |²⁴ expecting good weather,

but it rained all weekend. The last time Carl went camping he had a terrible time, too.

He | hasn't been   has been   wasn't |²⁵ having very good luck!

Score: _____

SIDE BY SIDE
Book 4

Student's Name _____   I.D. Number _____

Course _____   Teacher _____   Date _____

CHOOSE

Example:

A. Did Janet come to school on time today?
B. No. She _____ have overslept.
   a. should
   (b.) might
   c. couldn't
   d. mustn't

1. A. Grandpa moved his air conditioner by himself.
   B. I know. He's lucky. He _____ have broken his back.
   a. could
   b. couldn't
   c. should
   d. must

2. A. Did your brother do well on his science test?
   B. No. He _____ have studied more.
   a. couldn't
   b. must
   c. shouldn't
   d. should

3. A. Have your parents arrived at the party yet?
   B. No. They _____ have gotten lost.
   a. should
   b. must
   c. shouldn't
   d. mustn't

4. A. You look tired. Are you feeling okay?
   B. Yes, but I _____ have stayed up so late last night.
   a. shouldn't
   b. couldn't
   c. may
   d. could

5. A. How did Linda catch a cold?
   B. I'm not sure. She _____ have gone out in the rain.
   a. couldn't
   b. should
   c. may
   d. mustn't

CHOOSE

Example:

Mom didn't answer the phone. She _____ been sleeping.

a. should have
(b.) might have
c. hadn't
d. mustn't have

6. I think I ate too much at dinner. I definitely _____ skipped dessert.

a. should have
b. shouldn't have
c. had
d. must have

7. Lucy wasn't paying attention in class today. She _____ daydreaming.

a. couldn't be
b. must have been
c. should have been
d. must be

8. It's too bad you didn't practice for the marathon. You _____ won.

a. could have
b. may not have
c. must have
d. couldn't have

9. Jennifer _____ gone to the party last night. She should have done her homework instead.

a. couldn't have
b. must not have
c. hadn't
d. shouldn't have

10. My husband _____ in a car accident this morning. He's been at home all day.

a. shouldn't be
b. mustn't be
c. couldn't have been
d. shouldn't have been

CHOOSE

Example:

Nancy did very well on her history test. She must have studied _____.

a. more
b. a little
(c.) hard
d. too much

11. We couldn't hear our teacher at all today. She should have spoken _____.

a. harder
b. louder
c. softly
d. softer

12. Bill should have arrived _____. He could have missed the bus.

   a. earlier

   b. later

   c. faster

   d. slower

13. Gregory looks _____. He must have exercised a lot today.

   a. lonely

   b. irritable

   c. scared

   d. exhausted

14. You're _____. The weather was warm, and you could have fallen through the ice.

   a. tired

   b. lucky

   c. disappointed

   d. lonely

15. That dog must not have had its dinner. It looks very _____.

   a. hungry

   b. fat

   c. happy

   d. heavy

CHOOSE

Example:

Rachel caught a cold in the rain today. She must not have _____ a raincoat.

   (a.) worn

   b. left

   c. forgotten

   d. liked

16. Mark didn't have his textbook in class today. He may have _____.

   a. brought it

   b. left it at home

   c. been absent

   d. had it with him

17. Laura shouldn't have sold her house for that price. She could have _____ more money.

   a. sold it for

   b. bought

   c. wanted

   d. taken

18. Robert and Lisa had a terrible time at the beach. They should have _____ the mountains.

   a. returned from

   b. stayed

   c. gone to

   d. left

19. The neighbors haven't returned our ladder. They might have _____ it.

   a. taken

   b. gotten

   c. bought

   d. lost

20. James got fired yesterday. He shouldn't have _____.

   a. yelled at his boss

   b. arrived on time

   c. been in a good mood

   d. worked overtime

WHICH WORD?

No one knows why Harry arrived late for work this morning. Jonathan thinks he

should	(may)	mustn't

have been sick. Jennifer doesn't agree. She thinks he

couldn't	mustn't	might	21

have had car problems. But I think he

couldn't	must	should	22

have overslept because he *never* gets to bed on time.

Fortunately, his supervisor was in a good mood. Harry is very lucky. He

could	must	mustn't	23

have gotten fired. Still, I think Harry

couldn't	should	must	24

have called to say he wouldn't be on time, and he

shouldn't	couldn't	may	25

have gone to bed late!

Score: _____

Student's Name _____   I.D. Number _____

Course _____   Teacher _____   Date _____

CHOOSE

Example:

A. Do you want me to rewrite the report?
B. No. It's already _____.
   a. rewriting
   b. been rewriting
   (c.) been rewritten
   d. going to be rewritten

1. A. Has all the mail been distributed?
B. No. _____ yet.
   a. It's already been distributed
   b. It hasn't been distributed
   c. It's being distributed
   d. It's distributed

2. A. Should I sweep the floor?
B. Yes. _____.
   a. It hasn't been swept.
   b. It's been swept.
   c. It's being swept.
   d. It's going to be swept.

3. A. Who wrote this poem?
B. I think _____ by Maya Angelou.
   a. it's being written
   b. it has written
   c. it was written
   d. it will be written

4. A. Has my TV been repaired yet?
B. No. _____ right now.
   a. It's being repaired
   b. It hasn't been repaired
   c. It was repaired
   d. It wasn't repaired

5. A. What do you think about camping in public parks?
B. I don't think it _____ allowed.
   a. should have been
   b. shouldn't be
   c. must be
   d. should be

CHOOSE

Example:

That's the second time he's _____ this year.
(a.) been promoted
b. hurt
c. rejected
d. taken

6. My pants _____ by the tailor right now.
   a. are taking in
   b. have been taken in
   c. are being taken in
   d. were taken in

7. Construction of the new highway _____ a few months ago.

   a. has begun
   b. was begun
   c. has been begun
   d. will be begun

8. I'm very pleased. I think I'm going to _____ an important new position in my company.

   a. being offered
   b. be sent
   c. be taken
   d. be offered

9. This sonata _____ by Beethoven a long time ago.

   a. was composed
   b. has been composed
   c. composed
   d. is being composed

10. Last May Brian _____ by the Green Bay Company.

    a. had hired
    b. was hired
    c. has been hired
    d. was being hired

CHOOSE

Example:

I think this movie was _____ by Ingmar Bergman.

   a. drawn
   b. directed
   c. taken
   d. offered

11. Who was this magnificent mural _____ by?

    a. taken
    b. painted
    c. tuned up
    d. written

12. This is an impressive building. Who _____ it?

    a. designed
    b. invented
    c. considered
    d. composed

13. This skeleton was _____ last year by archeologists in Africa.

    a. made
    b. registered
    c. done
    d. found

14. Was that uniform _____ by the King of England?

    a. installed
    b. worn
    c. invented
    d. set

15. This casserole wasn't _____ by your son, was it?

    a. composed
    b. built
    c. made
    d. given out

CHOOSE

Example:

On her birthday, Amanda was given _____.

a. by her parents
(b.) many presents
c. her grandparents a present
d. a very exciting year

16. Joey was stung _____ bee.

a. as a
b. a
c. by a
d. from a

17. We were charged _____ for car repairs at Gary's Garage.

a. to the shop
b. a lot of money
c. by a lot of money
d. from the mechanics

18. I was invited _____ but I couldn't go.

a. by their house
b. their house
c. to them
d. to their house

19. Is it true that Max was offered _____ at the bakery?

a. a job
b. by the boss
c. as a baker
d. by a job

20. I don't think your native language should _____ during English class.

a. speak
b. be spoken
c. allow
d. been permitted

WHICH WORD?

This book [has (was) been] written by an author who has a very impressive

history. When she was only a teenager, her first short story [had been   been   was]²¹

published in a famous magazine. A few years later, when she was in college, she

[completed   was completed   has completed]²² her first novel, which was a story about a

dinosaur skeleton that a student [was   had   has]²³ discovered near a river in

China. Her next book [has been   was been   is being]²⁴ written now, but the details

[haven't   aren't   aren't being]²⁵ known yet.

Score: _____

Student's Name _____	I.D. Number _____
Course _____ Teacher _____	Date _____

CHOOSE

Example:

Can you tell me how much _____?

a. costs this suit
b. does this suit cost
c. this suit costs *(circled)*
d. does cost this suit

1. Do you have any idea how long _____ out?

a. had they been going
b. they had been going
c. did they go
d. were they going

2. Can you tell me why _____ closing early today?

a. is the store
b. does the store be
c. will the store be
d. the store is

3. How much money _____ last month?

a. we spent
b. spent we
c. did we spend
d. did we spent

4. Do you know _____ bitten by a cat or a dog?

a. if Alice was
b. was Alice
c. whether was Alice
d. if was Alice

5. When will you tell me what _____?

a. does that word mean
b. that word means
c. that word does mean
d. does mean that word

CHOOSE

Example:

Richard can't remember _____ last weekend.

a. what did he do
b. what he did *(circled)*
c. what was he doing
d. what had he done

6. My secretary doesn't remember _____ a copy of the letter.

a. if he gave me
b. did he give me
c. when did he give me
d. whether did he give me

7. Ethel has no idea _____ her new gloves.

   a. where did she put

   b. whether did she put

   c. where she put

   d. if she put

8. The real estate agent couldn't remember when _____.

   a. was their appointment

   b. their appointment was

   c. did they have an appointment

   d. if they had an appointment

9. Do you by any chance remember _____ those shoes?

   a. whether did you buy

   b. where did you buy

   c. when did you buy

   d. when you bought

10. William doesn't have any idea what _____.

   a. that movie was about

   b. was that movie about

   c. about was that movie

   d. about that movie was

CHOOSE

Example:

  A. Excuse me. Where is the bank?
  B. I'm sorry. I don't know _____.

   a. where is the bank

   (b.) where the bank is

   c. where's the bank

   d. where the bank

11. A. How can I get to Jim's house?
    B. I don't know. I'm not sure where _____.

   a. he lives

   b. does he live

   c. lives Jim

   d. is his house

12. A. Can we play soccer today?
    B. No. I don't think _____ soccer today.

   a. if you can play

   b. whether can you play

   c. you can play

   d. can you play

13. A. Was the security guard late today?
    B. I can't remember _____ on time or not.

   a. whether did he arrive

   b. if he arrived

   c. did he arrive

   d. if he did arrive

14. A. How often will you be away on business this year?
    B. I'm not sure how often _____ away.

   a. will I be

   b. if I'll be

   c. whether will I be

   d. I'll be

15. A. Is Berlin the capital of Germany?
    B. I'm not sure _____ the capital.

   a. what is

   b. if Berlin is

   c. whether is Berlin

   d. is Berlin

Student's Name _____	I.D. Number _____
Course _____ Teacher _____	Date _____

CHOOSE

Example:

If John _____ more time, he'd study more.

a. will have
(b.) had
c. has
d. had had

1. If our cat _____ friendlier, everyone would like him more.

a. were
b. be
c. will be
d. is

2. If it _____ a lot this winter, we'll probably go to Florida on vacation.

a. will snow
b. snowed
c. snows
d. won't snow

3. If Walter didn't enjoy his job, _____ work so hard.

a. he doesn't
b. he wouldn't
c. he'd
d. he won't

4. If you _____ too late, you might be very tired in the morning.

a. stayed up
b. don't stay up
c. can stay up
d. stay up

5. If Alexandra _____ another bad report card, her parents will be very angry.

a. gets
b. got
c. will get
d. might get

CHOOSE

Example:

If he weren't afraid, _____ willing to do it.

a. he's
b. he'll be
c. he was
d. he'd be *(circled)*

6. If we don't clean the environment, _____ better.

a. it'll get
b. it has gotten
c. it doesn't get
d. it won't get

7. If you don't get dressed up for the interview, _____ get the job.

a. you wouldn't
b. you'll
c. you might not
d. you couldn't

8. If she didn't have to study for a test, _____ to a movie with her friends.

a. she'll go
b. she'd go
c. she can go
d. she won't go

9. If Ralph doesn't work harder, _____ a promotion.

a. he won't get
b. he wouldn't get
c. he'll get
d. he might get

10. If they weren't absent so many times from school, _____ get better grades.

a. they'll
b. they'd
c. they might not
d. they wouldn't

CHOOSE

Example:

A. Is your husband satisfied with his job?
B. No, but if he _____, he'd like it more.

a. didn't get along with his boss
b. got a raise *(circled)*
c. works fewer hours
d. doesn't get a promotion

11. A. Are you going to move to a new city this year?
    B. _____. If we do, I'll miss my friends.

a. I hope so.
b. I hope not.
c. I don't hope so.
d. I hope.

CHOOSE

Example:

_____ almost there?

   a. Do you know if are we
   b. Can you tell me whether will we be
   ⓒ Do you by any chance know if we're
   d. Do you have any idea if are we

16. _____ vote for?

   a. Do you know who should I
   b. Can you tell me who I should
   c. Do you have any idea should I
   d. Do you have any idea who should I

17. _____ be back from her trip?

   a. Do you by any chance know when she'll
   b. Do you know if will she
   c. Could you please tell me when will she
   d. Can you tell me whether will she

18. _____ have to work this weekend?

   a. Do you know whether do you
   b. Can you tell me do you
   c. Do you have any idea if you
   d. Could you tell me do I

19. _____ going to stop raining.

   a. I'd like to know when is it
   b. I'm wondering when it's
   c. I'm not sure whether is it
   d. I don't know when is it

20. _____ that train comes by?

   a. Do you know how often does
   b. Can you tell me whether does
   c. Could you tell me when does
   d. Do you by any chance know how often

WHICH WORD?

My friend Marianne is thinking of traveling to Paris this fall, but she doesn't know

| is it | (if it's) | whether is it |

a good idea. First of all, she's never been to France, and

she has no idea | how | how does | if |²¹ the food tastes. Second, she used to have friends

in Paris, but she isn't sure | where do | where | whether |²² they live now. And finally,

Marianne can't speak French at all, and she doesn't have any idea

| who will she | if she'll | who she'll |²³ be able to communicate with.

On the other hand, everybody thinks Marianne should definitely go to France this fall

because she doesn't know | when she'll | when will she | whether will she |²⁴ have the

chance to go again, and she really doesn't have enough good reasons

| why shouldn't she | if she shouldn't | why she shouldn't |²⁵ go.

Score: _____

12. A. What should I do this weekend?
   B. Well, if _____, you can go to the beach.
   a. you don't want to go swimming
   b. the weather were sunny
   c. the park is closed
   d. you didn't have a lot of work to do

13. A. Why is Paul in such bad shape?
   B. He isn't concerned about his health. If _____, he'd exercise more.
   a. he were
   b. he did
   c. he is
   d. he were in bad shape

14. A. What would you do if your school were closed tomorrow?
   B. _____ probably go hiking.
   a. I might
   b. I'll
   c. I think I
   d. I'd

15. A. Has Albert been sick very long?
   B. No, but I _____ he gets better soon.
   a. think
   b. hope
   c. know
   d. hope so

CHOOSE

Example:

Diane hopes she gets _____ to college this fall.

a. paid
b. accessed
c. accepted
d. asked

16. I wonder why the police don't _____ that fight.

a. encourage
b. break up
c. break into
d. break out

17. They _____ hands all the time. I'm sure they're in love.

a. have
b. fold
c. hope
d. hold

18. Donald gets _____ every time he drives for more than an hour.

a. a raise
b. dressed up
c. carsick
d. there early

19. I hope the _____ from the factory doesn't get worse.

a. environment
b. pollution
c. profits
d. economy

20. If you _____ a coin in the wishing well, your wish will come true.

a. drop
b. drill
c. wish
d. fall

WHICH WORD?

I wonder what I [will   can   (would)] do if I lost my car keys in the morning

before work. If I [were   am   was]²¹ lucky, I'd find them right away. If not, I

[won't   wouldn't   can't]²² know what to do. I'd probably be late for work. If I'm

late for work again, I [might   might not   can't]²³ get fired. And if I

[weren't   shouldn't   didn't]²⁴ get fired, I'd at least get yelled at by my boss. If

I ever lose my car keys, I hope I [will find   find   won't find]²⁵ them quickly.

Score: _____

| Student's Name _____ | I.D. Number _____ |
| Course _____ Teacher _____ | Date _____ |

CHOOSE

Example:

A. Did Richard do well on his science test?
B. No. He _____ have studied more.
  a. couldn't
  b. must
  c. should *(circled)*
  d. mustn't

1. A. Should I make the beds?
B. No. They've _____ by your sister.
  a. been made
  b. made
  c. being made
  d. were made

2. A. Why didn't Carol come to the movie with us yesterday?
B. She _____ already seen it last week.
  a. hadn't
  b. has
  c. had been
  d. had

3. A. Your brother-in-law was very sick. How did he get better so quickly?
B. He was helped by a doctor _____ very well.
  a. that he has trained
  b. who had been trained
  c. which had been trained
  d. who trained him

4. A. Where is my calculator?
B. I don't know. Jim _____ have returned it yet.
  a. might not
  b. should not
  c. may
  d. must

5. A. Would you like to live in Europe someday?
B. No. If _____ there, I know I'd miss my friends.
  a. I live
  b. I had lived
  c. I lived
  d. I'm living

6. A. _____ you _____ watched TV for more than four hours?
B. Yes. In fact, I do every day.
  a. Did . . . ever
  b. Have . . . never
  c. Have . . . ever
  d. Didn't . . . never

7. A. What is our new neighbor's name?
B. Sorry. I don't remember _____.
  a. what is his name
  b. what his name is
  c. what's is his name
  d. what's his name is

8. A. _____ gone to the bank yet?
    B. Yes. _____ there a little while ago.
    a. Has she . . . She went
    b. Did she . . . She's gone
    c. Has she been . . . She went
    d. Was she . . . She's gone

9. A. I think I saw your son in the park earlier today.
    B. You _____ have. He's been away on business all week.
    a. shouldn't
    b. couldn't
    c. must
    d. could

10. A. Our classes might be canceled today.
    B. Really? If classes are canceled today, _____ very happy.
    a. I'm
    b. I can be
    c. I'll be
    d. will I be

11. A. Who wrote this symphony?
    B. I think it _____ by Beethoven a long time ago.
    a. wrote
    b. has been written
    c. had written
    d. was written

12. A. Was Joe on time for work this morning?
    B. No. He _____ have missed the bus.
    a. should
    b. must
    c. mustn't
    d. might not

13. A. Will the train be arriving soon?
    B. I'm not sure _____ be arriving soon.
    a. if whether it will
    b. if will it
    c. whether will it
    d. whether it will

14. A. Have your children been sick very long?
    B. Yes, they have. I _____ they get better soon.
    a. think
    b. hope
    c. hope so
    d. know

15. A. Have you seen Carl?
    B. No. He's _____ in his room all morning.
    a. sleeping
    b. been slept
    c. been sleeping
    d. has been sleeping

16. A. Jennifer doesn't feel very well.
    B. She _____ have eaten so much at dinner.
    a. shouldn't
    b. couldn't
    c. must not
    d. should

17. A. Would you like me to clean the living room?
    B. No. It _____ already _____ cleaned.
    a. was . . . being
    b. has . . . been
    c. hasn't . . . been
    d. has . . . being

18. A. It's too bad Harry was laid off last month.
    B. I know. _____ working for the company for many years.
        a. He's
        b. He was
        c. He had been
        d. He's been

19. A. Where is today's mail?
    B. It _____ yet.
        a. hasn't been delivered
        b. hasn't delivered
        c. didn't deliver
        d. has delivered

20. A. Do you think I should ride my motorcycle to work?
    B. No, I don't. _____ your motorcycle, I'm afraid _____ an accident.
        a. If you ride . . . you'll might have
        b. If you rode . . . you'll have
        c. If you ride . . . you'll have
        d. If you ride . . . you have

CHOOSE

Example:

If we _____ more time, we'd travel more often.
   a. had
   b. have had
   c. have
   d. haven't had

21. _____ has it been since it snowed?
    a. When
    b. How much
    c. How often
    d. How long

22. The customers _____ served by the waitress right now.
    a. have been
    b. were being
    c. are being
    d. are been

23. Mary didn't have an umbrella with her today. She _____ left it at home.
    a. may have
    b. should have
    c. hadn't
    d. should have

24. Do you know how much _____?
    a. costs it
    b. does it cost
    c. it costs
    d. if it costs

25. If we don't get lost, _____ be late for the party.
    a. we'll
    b. we won't
    c. we'd
    d. we're

26. Tina _____ just finished dessert when the phone rang.

   a. hadn't

   b. has

   c. had

   d. hasn't

27. All the windows _____ replaced recently _____ our landlord.

   a. have been . . . by

   b. have . . . by

   c. were being . . . for

   d. are . . . by

28. We were very lucky. We _____ have been injured.

   a. must

   b. will

   c. should

   d. could

29. If Timmy _____ so often, _____ better grades.

   a. didn't oversleep . . . he'll get

   b. overslept . . . he wouldn't get

   c. won't oversleep . . . he'll get

   d. didn't oversleep . . . he'd get

30. I can't remember _____.

   a. where did she work

   b. where she worked

   c. where has she worked

   d. where does she work

31. What had they been complaining about _____?

   a. just now

   b. since yesterday

   c. at that time

   d. next time

32. Sally _____ been sick last week. She didn't come to work.

   a. mustn't have

   b. might have

   c. should have

   d. hadn't

33. Do you know _____ their flight arrived on time?

   a. whether did

   b. when

   c. if

   d. did

34. I've been having problems with my computer _____ the past few weeks.

   a. for

   b. since

   c. until

   d. in

35. I've been looking at paintings _____.

   a. all morning

   b. when I arrived

   c. since three hours

   d. last night

36. If I _____ so much, _____ go on a diet.

   a. ate . . . I'd have to

   b. didn't eat . . . I wouldn't have to

   c. eat . . . I'll have to

   d. didn't eat . . . I'll

37. The police said our music _____ so loudly.

   a. should play

   b. shouldn't play

   c. should be played

   d. shouldn't be played

38. That famous author _____ written many books before he died.

    a. had been

    b. has

    c. was

    d. had

39. Do you know what _____ since he left the company?

    a. he's been doing

    b. he's working

    c. does he work

    d. he does

40. _____ enough money, _____ pay off all my debts.

    a. If I had . . . I'll

    b. If I have . . . I'd

    c. If I had . . . I'd

    d. If I'll have . . . I'd

WHICH WORD?

For several weeks last (summer)   weekend   night , George's friends had been

telling him to open up a Greek restaurant. George [wanted   has wanted   wants] [41]

to open a restaurant last summer, but he [wasn't able to be   was   wasn't] [42] sure

[was it   if it was   whether was it] [43] a good idea for a few reasons.

First of all, he doesn't know [anything   if   how] [44] to cook Greek food.

Also, he [didn't   hadn't   hasn't] [45] have enough money at that time.

Recently a Greek restaurant [opened   was opened   opens] [46] by someone else,

and it [was   is   has] [47] become very successful. George is upset. He knows he

[should   must   may] [48] have opened a restaurant himself. And he knows it

[mustn't   shouldn't   could] [49] have been successful. If he opens a different

restaurant now, maybe [he'll   he has to   he'd] [50] be rich someday.

Score: _____

CHOOSE

Example:

Bruce wishes he _____ better.

(a.) could cook
b. cooks
c. can cook
d. was cooking

1. Mr. and Mrs. Lee _____ they can take a vacation soon.

a. hope so
b. wish
c. will hope
d. hope

2. Angela wishes she _____ a more interesting job.

a. has
b. had
c. can have
d. might have

3. Albert _____ it doesn't rain this afternoon.

a. wishes
b. knows
c. hopes
d. thinks

4. My sister can play the guitar, but she wishes she _____ the piano.

a. can play
b. didn't play
c. could play
d. plays

5. Timothy wishes _____ as athletic as his older brother.

a. he were
b. he was
c. he's
d. he can be

CHOOSE

Example:

I _____ order the chicken if I were you.

a. shouldn't
(b.) wouldn't
c. won't
d. couldn't

6. If Marty _____ get a full-time job, he'd make a lot more money.

a. didn't
b. hopes to
c. could
d. wishes to

7. Do you think my supervisor _____ be upset if I refused to work overtime this weekend?

   a. would
   b. will
   c. won't
   d. can

8. If Marilyn were able to knit, she'd _____ make a sweater for her grandson.

   a. could
   b. be able to
   c. wishes to
   d. can

9. Do you think my boyfriend will be jealous if _____ dinner with John this Saturday night?

   a. I've
   b. I had
   c. I have
   d. I've had

10. My wife has to work the late shift tonight. She wishes she _____.

   a. did
   b. won't
   c. doesn't
   d. didn't

CHOOSE

Example:

Could you get some baby _____ at the store?

   (a.) food
   b. picture
   c. children
   d. cookie

11. I'm thinking of taking a _____ next fall.

   a. classified ad
   b. driver's ed
   c. foreign language
   d. doctor's appointment

12. Our landlord has been raising our _____ every year for the past five years.

   a. rent
   b. taxes
   c. water
   d. repairs

13. I would be willing to do it, but I don't have enough _____ time.

   a. busy
   b. over
   c. part
   d. spare

14. Frank was _____ his apartment because he made too much noise.

   a. dropped out of
   b. evicted from
   c. jealous of
   d. left from

15. How long have you been _____ each other?

   a. angry
   b. going out with
   c. jealous
   d. going out

CHOOSE

Example:

You should be careful about starting an Internet company. You might _____.

a. have all heart
b. keep your chin up
(c.) lose your shirt
d. be able to

16. Oliver has "two left feet." He wishes he _____.

a. could dance better
b. knew how to fix things
c. could run faster
d. had two right feet

17. Richard can't _____ French as well as his sister. She has a better ear for languages.

a. read
b. listen to
c. speak
d. study

18. It's too _____ in this apartment building. I wish there were more peace and quiet.

a. upset
b. angry
c. quiet
d. noisy

19. I'm sick and tired of the rainy weather. I _____ soon.

a. should call a doctor
b. hope it gets sunny
c. will get better
d. hope it rains

20. George can never fix anything around the house. He's _____.

a. handy
b. got a green thumb
c. all thumbs
d. mechanically inclined

WHICH WORD?

Sharon [hopes   knows   (wishes)] she had a part-time job. If she

[has   had   did]²¹ a part-time job, she'd have more money to spend. But right now,

she's a full-time student, and she's very busy with her classes. If I were Sharon, I

[wouldn't   won't   don't]²² get a part-time job. If she got one, she

[can   might   won't]²³ have more money, but [she's   she'd   she could]²⁴ have a

lot less time to study. And if she doesn't spend enough time studying, she

[won't   might   wouldn't]²⁵ get good grades.

Score: _____

Student's Name		I.D. Number
Course	Teacher	Date

CHOOSE

Example:

I lived in the suburbs when I was young, but _____ in the city.

- **(a.)** I wish I had lived
- b. I wished I lived
- c. I wish I live
- d. I wish I didn't live

1. _____ lost on the way to the party. We were two hours late.

   - a. I wish we didn't get
   - b. I wish we hadn't gotten
   - c. I wish we haven't gotten
   - d. I wish we weren't

2. Mrs. Banks didn't plant any flowers last spring. Now it's summer, and _____ some.

   - a. she wishes she were planting
   - b. she hopes she planted
   - c. she hopes she had planted
   - d. she wishes she had planted

3. My grandmother _____ her more often. She misses me a lot.

   - a. wishes I visited
   - b. wishes I visit
   - c. hopes I had visited
   - d. hopes I visited

4. Ronald _____ more when he was in high school.

   - a. wishes he had been studied
   - b. hopes he studied
   - c. wishes he had studied
   - d. hopes he had studied

5. _____ at that traffic light. I wouldn't have been given a ticket by a police officer.

   - a. I hope I stopped
   - b. I wish I had stopped
   - c. I wish I stopped
   - d. I hope I had stopped

CHOOSE

Example:

If _____ you were hungry, I would have made more for dinner.

- a. I knew
- **(b.)** I had known
- c. I know
- d. I didn't know

6. If _____ searched by the security person at the airport, I'm going to be upset.

   - a. I get
   - b. I got
   - c. I didn't get
   - d. I had gotten

7. If Larry hadn't overslept, _____ an hour late for the meeting.

   a. he wouldn't be
   b. he won't be
   c. he must not have been
   d. he wouldn't have been

8. If Kelly _____ enough sleep last night, she wouldn't be so irritable today.

   a. had gotten
   b. wouldn't get
   c. got
   d. didn't get

9. We would invite you to dinner if _____ us more often.

   a. you would have called
   b. you called
   c. you've called
   d. you hadn't called

10. If I hadn't been prepared, I know _____ done well on my physics test.

    a. I would have
    b. I must have
    c. I wouldn't have
    d. I wouldn't had

CHOOSE

Example:

   A. I wonder why our teacher didn't come to class yesterday.
   B. _____ sick.
      a. She must not be
      b. She wouldn't have been
      c. She must have been
      d. She wouldn't be

11. A. It's a shame you get depressed so often.
    B. I know. _____ an optimist.
       a. I hope I'm
       b. I had wished I'm
       c. I wish I were
       d. I wish I'm

12. A. Why didn't Joe get the job?
    B. If _____ late for the interview, he probably would have been hired.
       a. he wasn't
       b. he had been
       c. he isn't
       d. he hadn't been

13. A. I wonder why Sam is so unhappy.
    B. His girlfriend _____ broken up with him.
       a. would have
       b. must have
       c. wishes he had
       d. hopes she had

14. A. Will Irene take a vacation this fall?
    B. I'm not sure. But if she does, _____ me a postcard.
       a. I hope she sends
       b. I wish she had sent
       c. I hope she had sent
       d. I hope she sent

15. A. Why don't you come to the park with us this afternoon?
    B. If I go to the park, _____ my work.
       a. I wouldn't have finished
       b. I must have finished
       c. I won't finish
       d. I hope I had finished

CHOOSE

Example:

If they had seen us, _____ to say hello.

a. they wouldn't have run by
b. they would stop
(c.) they would have stopped
d. they stopped

16. If Walter walks to work today, _____ his umbrella.

a. I hope he takes
b. I wish he took
c. I wish he takes
d. I wish he had taken

17. If Susan didn't have to go to bed, _____ shut down her computer.

a. she must not have
b. she doesn't have to
c. she wishes she had
d. she wouldn't have to

18. If Dad had had the right ingredients, I'm sure _____ cookies for us.

a. he could make
b. he would have made
c. he'd make
d. he'll make

19. I wish it had been sunny at the beach. _____ a better time.

a. We would have
b. We would have had
c. We hope we had had
d. We had had

20. If I had a better job, _____ so concerned about my future.

a. I wouldn't be
b. I wouldn't have been
c. I wasn't
d. I'm sure I won't be

WHICH WORD?

There's a rumor that our neighbors are going to move, but I | wish   wished   (hope) |

it isn't true. If they move, my wife and I will | have to find   have found   met |²¹

some new friends. However, unfortunately, I think the rumor is true. If our neighbors

| hadn't moved   weren't going to move   didn't move |²² they probably

| had sold   wouldn't have sold   wouldn't sell |²³ most of their furniture last week.

Our neighbors | had been   must be   wish they're |²⁴ very busy these days because

otherwise I'm sure they | will tell   had told   would have told |²⁵ us they were going to

leave the neighborhood.

Score: _____

Student's Name _____   I.D. Number _____

Course _____   Teacher _____   Date _____

CHOOSE

Example:

Howard told us _____ popular music.

a. if he didn't like
b. he didn't like
c. if he likes
d. whether did he like

1. We had no idea that your daughter Sarah _____ a doctor someday.

   a. had been going to be
   b. has been
   c. wanted to be
   d. had been

2. The landlord called and said _____ our kitchen sink by 3 o'clock today.

   a. he's able to fix
   b. he would be able to fix
   c. he's fixed
   d. if he'll fix

3. Our teacher said we couldn't use our dictionaries, but she didn't say _____ use our textbooks during the test.

   a. we couldn't
   b. we can
   c. were we able to
   d. if we can

4. I asked George to come with us to the beach tomorrow, but he said _____ too busy.

   a. he's been
   b. he had been
   c. he was
   d. he won't be

5. I had no idea _____ our office in Detroit.

   a. they were going to close
   b. they're going to close
   c. are they going to close
   d. if they're closing

6. Aunt Peggy can't come over today, but she said _____ us soon.

   a. she'll visit
   b. she had visited
   c. she's visiting
   d. she would visit

7. In their letter, they said _____ us.

   a. they missed
   b. if they missed
   c. they're missing
   d. had they missed

8. Our son Thomas told us _____ engaged soon.

   a. he had gotten
   b. if he had gotten
   c. he got
   d. he was getting

9. She told them the reason she couldn't go to the meeting last Friday was that _____ sick all that week.

a. whether she was

b. she's been

c. she had been

d. she's

10. We were unaware _____ moved away.

a. had they

b. they had

c. if they had

d. whether they

CHOOSE

Example:

A woman on the street asked me _____.

a. where was the bus station

b. where the bus station was

c. where is the bus station

d. where's the bus station

11. At my job interview, I was asked _____ been looking for work.

a. how long had I

b. how long have I

c. how long I had

d. whether had I

12. Did they ask you _____ qualified for the job?

a. if you were

b. were you

c. why were you

c. whether were you

13. I _____ your room, but you haven't done it yet.

a. told to you to clean

b. said to have cleaned

c. told you to clean

d. said you to clean

14. The police told them _____ their neighbors anymore.

a. don't bother

b. to not bother

c. not bother

d. not to bother

15. My boss asked me _____ the door to the store.

a. did I lock

b. if I had locked

c. if did I lock

d. I had locked

16. She asked me _____ this weekend.

a. what I was going to do

b. what was I going to do

c. was I busy

d. what am I going to do

17. My teacher asked me _____.

a. where was my homework

b. where is my homework

c. where my homework was

d. where my homework is

18. They told all the employees _____ early tomorrow.

    a. to come to work

    b. not come to work

    c. whether to not come to work

    d. don't come to work

19. My parents asked me _____ to marry Jerry.

    a. if had I decided

    b. if I had decided

    c. did I decide

    d. whether did I decide

20. Her teacher asked her _____ hard for the test.

    a. if did she study

    b. if had she studied

    c. if did she study

    d. if she had studied

WHICH WORD?

Last night my sister called from London and asked [if   whether   (what)] was new.

She said that since she [is   had been   was]²¹ away from home for so long she

[isn't   had been   wasn't]²² aware how everyone was. I told her that we all missed

her and that we [are   were   would be]²³ wondering when she would come back.

Then she said that she didn't know whether [she would   she'll   would she]²⁴ come back

at all because she [would be   was   been]²⁵ very happy living in England.

Score: _____

Student's Name _____ I.D. Number _____

Course _____ Teacher _____ Date _____

CHOOSE

Example:

Your daughter Janet took the
SAT test last week, _____?

  a. doesn't she
  (b.) didn't she
  c. did she
  d. isn't she

1. They've already gotten engaged, _____?

  a. didn't they
  b. have they
  c. haven't they
  d. did they

2. You hadn't seen them before, _____?

  a. had you
  b. have you
  c. hadn't you
  d. had they

3. She's been promoted several times
this year, _____?

  a. isn't she
  b. hasn't she
  c. didn't she
  d. is she

4. I'm not disturbing you, _____?

  a. am I
  b. do I
  c. are you
  d. aren't you

5. He's trying to discover a cure for
he common cold, _____?

  a. doesn't he
  b. hasn't he
  c. does he
  d. isn't he

CHOOSE

Example:

Edward _____ transferred to our
office in Cleveland, is he?

  a. is going to be
  (b.) isn't going to be
  c. doesn't want to be
  d. hasn't been

6. _____ complaining too much, aren't I!

  a. I'm
  b. You're
  c. I are
  d. I'm not

7. They _____ quite a few problems the year before, hadn't they!

   a. had
   b. had had
   c. hadn't had
   d. didn't have

8. Mr. Lewis _____ whether we were allergic to milk, wasn't he?

   a. asked
   b. wasn't asking
   c. was wondering
   d. wasn't aware

9. Those cookies _____ eaten by your brother, will they?

   a. won't be
   b. willn't be
   c. won't being
   d. will be

10. _____ allowed to play frisbee inside the house, am I?

   a. I aren't
   b. I won't be
   c. I'd not
   d. I'm not

CHOOSE

Example:

   A. This food _____ bad.
   B. I agree. This food DOES taste bad, doesn't it!
      a. does
      (b.) tastes
      c. doesn't taste
      d. isn't too

11. A. That man _____ very polite to us.
    B. You're right. He hasn't, has he!
      a. wasn't
      b. isn't being
      c. has been
      d. hasn't been

12. A. My daughter is very smart. She can count to ten by herself.
    B. She _____?!
      a. does
      b. can
      c. can't
      d. is

13. A. I think our pets are the friendliest pets in the neighborhood.
    B. Yes, _____!
      a. I DON'T, do I
      b. they DO, don't they
      c. they ARE, aren't they
      d. they AREN'T, are they

14. A. Jennifer _____ careful when she types.
    B. Yes, she DOES, doesn't she!
      a. doesn't try to be
      b. is trying to be
      c. always tries to be
      d. isn't trying to be

15. A. That's not very considerate of you.
    B. You're right. It _____!
      a. IS, isn't it
      b. ISN'T, is it
      c. HASN'T, has it
      d. HAS, hasn't it

CHOOSE

Example:

Nancy is always _____ because she hates being late.

(a.) punctual
b. dedicated
c. polite
d. patient

16. That was the _____ ride we've ever been on, wasn't it!

a. scariest
b. most frightened
c. shocked
d. most surprised

17. The students think it's really _____ that our English teacher gave us so much homework this weekend.

a. angry
b. generous
c. unfair
d. unhappy

18. I hope I get _____ this month. I need the money.

a. engaged
b. prepared
c. generous
d. promoted

19. Ben was _____ when his girlfriend broke their engagement.

a. honest
b. shocked
c. industrious
d. disturbing

20. Maria works very quickly and accurately. She's the most _____ person in our office.

a. cooperative
b. considerate
c. thoughtful
d. efficient

WHICH WORD?

My friend Henry got a phone call from his girlfriend Susan that made him very

| (upset) | unusual | exciting |

. During the call, she said that Henry had been late for

their dates too often, but Henry feels that he | isn't | hasn't been | has been |²¹ late too

often. Susan also said that he spent too much time at work, but Henry disagrees. He really

| does | doesn't | hasn't |²² spend too much time at work. Then she asked him why

he couldn't be more considerate, and Henry said that he | has | can | was |²³

very considerate. Finally, Susan said that she didn't think he loved her, but Henry

disagreed. He maintains that he | doesn't | does | has |²⁴ love her.

Henry and Susan realize that they should talk about their problems. If they don't, they'll

probably break up soon, | won't | will | shouldn't |²⁵ they!

Score: _____

| Student's Name _____ | I.D. Number _____ |
| Course _____ Teacher _____ | Date _____ |

CHOOSE

Example:

_____ your computer was broken,
I would have helped you.

a. If I knew
b. **If I had known**
c. If I've known
d. If I hadn't known

1. _____ to Mexico next month, we'll buy
you a present.

a. If we go
b. If we went
b. If we'd go
c. If we had gone

2. If Charles didn't work out every day,
_____ overweight.

a. he wouldn't be
b. he won't be
c. he'd be
d. he'll be

3. If you give me a message, of course
_____ it down.

a. I'd write
b. I'll write
c. I'd written
d. I've written

4. _____ to your advice, this wouldn't
have happened.

a. If I listened
b. If I'll listen
c. If I wouldn't listen
d. If I had listened

5. If I hadn't eaten so much food, _____
a lot better.

a. I'd feel
b. I'll feel
c. I'm sure I'll
d. I had felt

CHOOSE

Example:

_____ so busy, I'd be happy to
go with you.

a. **If I weren't**
b. If I wasn't
c. If I hadn't been
d. If I won't be

6. I suppose _____ trouble if you tried
to do that by yourself.

a. you'd have
b. you'll have
c. you had had
d. you won't have

7. I'm afraid I can't help you right now. _____ my sick dog to the vet yet.

    a. I have to

    b. I hadn't taken

    c. I haven't taken

    d. I'm taking

8. I'm going to take chemistry next semester. _____ I don't fail the course.

    a. I'd hope

    b. I hope

    c. I wish

    d. I'll hope

9. If our dog _____ very hungry, he wouldn't have eaten the cat food.

    a. won't have been

    b. wouldn't have been

    c. shouldn't have been

    d. hadn't been

10. How long _____ trouble communicating with each other?

    a. hadn't they had

    b. have they been having

    c. had they've had

    d. are they having

CHOOSE

Example:

The truth is, I really don't _____ any videos.

    a. get tired to watch

    (b.) feel like watching

    c. feel like to watch

    d. feel to watch

11. My family _____ to get new wallpaper for our house.

    a. is insisting us

    b. is urging us

    c. is about to

    d. is misunderstanding us

12. Don't you ever get tired _____ your batteries?

    a. to use

    b. to replace

    c. of replacing

    d. to figure out

13. Would you like _____ assemble my new desk?

    a. help me

    b. helping me

    c. you to help

    d. to help me

14. Are you having trouble _____ your income tax return?

    a. filling out

    b. to fill out

    c. working

    d. to be working on

15. How long _____ the lock on your front door?

    a. did you replace

    b. can you set up

    c. has he refused to fix

    d. can you change

CHOOSE

Example:

If I _____ shopping yesterday, _____ happy to go shopping today.

  a. hadn't gone . . . I'll be

  (b.) hadn't gone . . . I'd be

  c. had gone . . . I wouldn't be

  d. didn't go . . . I'll be

16. _____ you had to work overtime tonight, _____ asked you to go to the movies with me.

  a. If I had known . . . I'd have

  b. If I hadn't known . . . I would have

  c. If I had known . . . I wouldn't have

  d. If I hadn't known . . . I wouldn't have

17. _____ hit the right key, _____ deleted all your files.

  a. If you had . . . you wouldn't have

  b. If you don't . . . you will

  c. If you . . . you wouldn't have

  d. If you hadn't . . . you

18. _____ sick in bed, _____ glad to help you move this weekend.

  a. If I was . . . I wouldn't be

  b. If I were . . . I'll be

  c. If I hadn't been . . . I was

  d. If I weren't . . . I'd be

19. _____ misunderstood the directions, _____ gotten lost.

  a. If I had . . . I wouldn't have

  b. If I . . . I'd have

  c. If I hadn't . . . I wouldn't have

  d. If I had . . . I had

20. _____ lost your balance, you _____ fallen.

  a. If you . . . wouldn't have

  b. If you hadn't . . . wouldn't have

  c. If you had . . . had

  d. If you had . . . wouldn't have

WHICH WORD?

Pamela wishes she ⌈ didn't listen   has listened   (had listened) ⌉ to her friends' advice

before she bought her house. They told her that if she bought that house, she would probably

⌈ regret   have regretted   had regretted ⌉²¹ it, and she does.

Since she moved in a few months ago ⌈ she's   she'd   she'll ⌉²² had to call

the plumber to repair the pipes several times. Also, she's caught a cold three times

because she's been having trouble ⌈ gotten   to get   getting ⌉²³ the heater to work.

Pamela's friends told her that the house ⌈ has been   was   had been ⌉²⁴ too old,

but she didn't listen. If she had only listened, she ⌈ must   will   would ⌉²⁵ never

have bought it!

Score: _____

Student's Name _____ I.D. Number _____

Course _____ Teacher _____ Date _____

CHOOSE

Example:

A. I wonder why Alan didn't come to work on time this morning.
B. He _____ have missed the train.
   a. wouldn't
   (b.) must
   c. should
   d. mustn't

1. A. Why won't you come to the movies with us this afternoon?
   B. If I go to the movies with you, _____ all the work I have to do.
   a. I wish I had finished
   b. I won't finish
   c. I mustn't have finished
   d. I wouldn't finish

2. A. I didn't want to come to school today.
   B. If you hadn't come, you _____ missed the test.
   a. would have
   b. had
   c. hadn't
   d. must have

3. A. John _____ very carefully.
   B. You're right. He DOES, doesn't he!
   a. is driving
   b. has been driving
   c. drives
   d. doesn't drive

4. A. Why can't you come over now?
   B. I _____ my paper yet.
   a. hadn't written
   b. have to write
   c. am writing
   d. haven't written

5. A. Cindy is tired of walking to work.
   B. If she got a car, she _____ to drive there.
   a. would have
   b. would be able
   c. could be able
   d. will be able

6. A. What did Jim ask you?
   B. He asked me _____ put his car keys.
   a. where I had
   b. if I had
   c. to
   d. where did I

7. A. Janet is very unhappy at the company.
   B. That's too bad. She won't quit her job, _____?
   a. won't she
   b. doesn't she
   c. will she
   d. would she

8. A. Your sister's car isn't working well these days.
    B. I know. I've been urging her _____ a new one.
    a. of buying
    b. buy
    c. in buying
    d. to buy

9. A. Why aren't you having any dessert?
    B. My doctor told me _____ any cake or ice cream.
    a. don't eat
    b. to not have
    c. not to have
    d. to have

10. A. Have you heard from your cousin Tom?
    B. Yes. He told us _____ us soon.
    a. he'll visit
    b. he had visited
    c. if he would visit
    d. he was going to visit

11. A. If we _____ to Hong Kong next year, will you come with us?
    B. I'd love to go with you.
    a. go
    b. went
    c. are going
    d. had gone

12. A. I didn't know that you _____ play the violin.
    B. Yes, and I can play the cello, too.
    a. are able to
    b. couldn't
    c. were able to
    d. can't

13. A. Why didn't you have a good time on your vacation?
    B. The weather was bad. If the weather _____ nice, we _____ a better time.
    a. were . . . would have
    b. had been . . . would have had
    c. hadn't been . . . would have had
    d. were . . . had had

14. A. My mother thinks you're too quiet.
    B. I'm not too quiet, _____ I?
    a. are
    b. am
    c. aren't
    d. amn't

15. A. What were you just doing in my office?
    B. I _____ for my notebook.
    a. have looked
    b. am looking
    c. was looking
    d. had been looking

16. A. Does Michael regret being a lawyer?
    B. Yes. He _____ become a teacher.
    a. wished he
    b. wishes he has
    c. hopes he has
    d. wishes he had

17. A. Has Karen ever been to Europe?
    B. No. But if she saved enough money, _____ go there someday.
    a. she can
    b. she'll
    c. she would have to
    d. she could

18. A. Daniel has gotten a little heavy.
    B. I know. He's on a diet. _____ he can lose some weight.
       a. He wishes
       b. He hopes
       c. He's trying
       d. He wished

19. A. What did that man ask you?
    B. He asked me _____ downtown.
       a. where does this bus go
       b. does this bus go
       c. whether this bus goes
       d. if does this bus go

20. A. I think our teacher gives us too much homework.
    B. I agree. She _____, _____!
       a. doesn't . . . does she
       b. does . . . doesn't she
       c. doesn't . . . doesn't she
       d. does . . . does she

CHOOSE

Example:

If _____ the day shift, I'd be able to spend more time with my kids.

a. I worked
b. I'll work
c. I work
d. I had worked

21. You weren't going to eat that, _____ you?
    a. didn't
    b. did
    c. were
    d. weren't

22. The lawyer asked me _____ late for our appointment next week.
    a. not to be
    b. to stop being
    c. to be not
    d. to stop to be

23. Do you think my children will be disappointed _____ to the zoo this weekend?
    a. if we haven't gone
    b. we went
    c. if we don't go
    d. whether we went

24. If Mark _____ the job, I'm sure he would have called.
    a. would get
    b. had gotten
    c. gets
    d. will get

25. Howard went fishing yesterday, but he told everybody _____ sick.
    a. he was
    b. to be sick
    c. he has been
    d. he's

26. I wish I had known more people at the party. _____ a better time.

   a. I would have

   b. I would have had

   c. I hope I had had

   d. I had had

27. My piano teacher asked me _____.

   a. how long had I practiced

   b. how long did I practice

   c. how long I had practiced

   d. whether did I practice

28. Did the doctor tell you _____?

   a. what was the problem

   b. what's the problem

   c. whether was it a problem

   d. what the problem was

29. I don't really _____ doing the laundry right now.

   a. want to

   b. feel to

   c. feel like

   d. in the mood

30. She'd tell us if she spoke French, _____ she?

   a. didn't

   b. wouldn't

   c. hadn't

   d. will

31. I'm afraid I can't help you fix your air conditioner right now. _____ breakfast yet.

   a. I have to have

   b. I haven't had

   c. I hadn't had

   d. I'm having

32. If you had told me to feed the cat, I certainly _____ it.

   a. can do

   b. would do

   c. will do

   d. would have done

33. My guests asked me _____ the dessert myself.

   a. if had I made

   b. if I had made

   c. did I make

   d. whether did I make

34. Do you often have trouble _____ names?

   a. to be remembering

   b. to have remembered

   c. remembering

   d. to be remembered

35. I had no idea _____ to move to the suburbs this summer.

   a. you're planning

   b. you were planning

   c. if you're planning

   d. had you been planning

36. I never _____ that if I _____ any idea it would make me sick.

   a. would eat . . . have

   b. had eaten . . . had had

   c. would have eaten . . . had had

   d. ate . . . had

37. I didn't realize _____ to work overtime this weekend.

   a. everybody had been asked

   b. the boss has asked us

   c. if we were asked

   d. had we been asked

38. You've never met them before, _____ you?

    a. aren't

    b. are

    c. have

    d. did

39. If we _____ able to, we'd come to your wedding.

    a. would be

    b. were

    c. are

    d. could be

40. Jerry told _____ after five o'clock.

    a. me to call

    b. he was free

    c. you were busy

    d. to call me

WHICH WORD?

When Michael | has been   went   (was) | in college ten years ago, he decided

| study   studying   to study |⁴¹ German. At the time, he thought

| had it been   it was   it's been |⁴² a good idea, but now he isn't sure he made the right

decision.

Last month Michael had an interview for a wonderful job in Italy, but he wasn't hired. If

| he   he had   he has |⁴³ studied Italian in college, he thinks he might have gotten the

job. Then last Saturday he was asked | if he would   whether will he   if he can |⁴⁴

come to an international party. When he got there, everybody was speaking Spanish,

(continued)

Japanese, Korean, and Chinese, and no one was speaking German! If Michael had studied one

of those languages in college, he definitely | would have   had had   would have had |⁴⁵

more fun at the party. Then this morning, he met a very interesting French girl at a café. If he

had studied French in college, he | had   must have   might have |⁴⁶ asked her to go on

a date this weekend.

     Michael is upset now. He | hopes he had   wishes he had   wishes he has |⁴⁷ learned

another language. If he had known he wouldn't use German, he definitely

| would have   hadn't   wouldn't have |⁴⁸ studied it. In fact, he told me he

| was   is   would be |⁴⁹ going to start learning a new language next week. However, he

said he | hasn't   couldn't   won't |⁵⁰ decide which language to study!

Score: _____

CHAPTER 1

CHOOSE

1. a	4. d
2. b	5. d
3. c	

CHOOSE

6. a	9. b
7. c	10. d
8. a	

CHOOSE

11. c	14. d
12. a	15. b
13. b	

CHOOSE

16. c	19. b
17. a	20. b
18. d	

WHICH WORD?

21. he had
22. bought
23. had
24. had been
25. hasn't been

CHAPTER 2

CHOOSE

1. a	4. a
2. d	5. c
3. b	

CHOOSE

6. a	9. d
7. b	10. c
8. a	

CHOOSE

11. b	14. b
12. a	15. a
13. d	

CHOOSE

16. b	19. d
17. a	20. a
18. c	

WHICH WORD?

21. might
22. must
23. could
24. should
25. shouldn't

CHAPTER 3

CHOOSE

1. b	4. a
2. a	5. d
3. c	

CHOOSE

6. c	9. a
7. b	10. b
8. d	

CHOOSE

11. b	14. b
12. a	15. c
13. d	

CHOOSE

16. c	19. a
17. b	20. b
18. d	

WHICH WORD?

21. was
22. completed
23. had
24. is being
25. aren't

CHAPTER 4

CHOOSE

1. b	4. a
2. d	5. b
3. c	

CHOOSE

6. a	9. d
7. c	10. a
8. b	

CHOOSE

11. a	14. d
12. c	15. b
13. b	

CHOOSE

16. b	19. b
17. a	20. d
18. c	

WHICH WORD?

21. how
22. where
23. who she'll
24. when she'll
25. why she shouldn't

CHAPTER 5

CHOOSE

1. a	4. d
2. c	5. a
3. b	

CHOOSE

6. d	9. a
7. c	10. b
8. b	

CHOOSE

11. b	14. d
12. c	15. b
13. a	

CHOOSE

16. b	19. b
17. d	20. a
18. c	

WHICH WORD?

21. were
22. wouldn't
23. might
24. didn't
25. find

MID-BOOK TEST

CHOOSE

1. a	11. d
2. d	12. b
3. b	13. d
4. a	14. b
5. c	15. c
6. c	16. a
7. b	17. b
8. a	18. c
9. b	19. a
10. c	20. c

CHOOSE

21. d	31. c
22. c	32. b
23. a	33. c
24. c	34. a
25. b	35. a
26. c	36. b
27. a	37. d
28. d	38. d
29. d	39. a
30. b	40. c

WHICH WORD?

41. wanted
42. wasn't
43. if it was
44. how
45. didn't
46. was opened
47. has
48. should
49. could
50. he'll

CHAPTER 6

CHOOSE

1. d	4. c
2. b	5. a
3. c	

CHOOSE

6. c	9. c
7. a	10. d
8. b	

CHOOSE

11. c	14. b
12. a	15. b
13. d	

CHOOSE

16. a	19. b
17. c	20. c
18. d	

WHICH WORD?

21. had
22. wouldn't
23. might
24. she'd
25. won't

CHAPTER 7

CHOOSE

1. b	4. c
2. d	5. b
3. a	

CHOOSE

6. a	9. b
7. d	10. c
8. a	

CHOOSE

11. c	14. a
12. d	15. c
13. b	

CHOOSE

16. a	19. b
17. d	20. a
18. b	

WHICH WORD?

21. have to find
22. weren't going to move
23. wouldn't have sold
24. must be
25. would have told

CHAPTER 8

CHOOSE

1. c	6. d
2. b	7. a
3. a	8. d
4. c	9. c
5. a	10. b

CHOOSE

11. c	16. a
12. a	17. c
13. c	18. a
14. d	19. b
15. b	20. d

WHICH WORD?

21. had been
22. wasn't
23. were
24. she would
25. was

CHAPTER 9

CHOOSE

1. c	4. a
2. a	5. d
3. b	

CHOOSE

6. a	9. a
7. b	10. d
8. c	

CHOOSE

11. d	14. c
12. b	15. b
13. c	

CHOOSE

16. a	19. b
17. c	20. d
18. d	

WHICH WORD?

21. hasn't been
22. doesn't
23. was
24. does
25. won't

CHAPTER 10

CHOOSE

1. a	4. d
2. c	5. a
3. b	

Choose

6. a
7. c
8. b
9. d
10. b

Choose

11. b
12. c
13. d
14. a
15. c

Choose

16. c
17. a
18. d
19. c
20. b

Which Word?

21. regret
22. she's
23. getting
24. was
25. would

FINAL TEST

Choose

1. b
2. a
3. c
4. d
5. b
6. a
7. c
8. d
9. c
10. d
11. a
12. c
13. b
14. b
15. c
16. d
17. d
18. b
19. c
20. b
21. c
22. a
23. c
24. b
25. a
26. b
27. c
28. d
29. c
30. b
31. b
32. d
33. b
34. c
35. b
36. c
37. a
38. c
39. b
40. a

Which Word?

41. to study
42. it was
43. he had
44. if he would
45. would have had
46. might have
47. wishes he had
48. wouldn't have
49. was
50. couldn't

SIDE BY SIDE
Chapter Test Answer Sheet

BOOK _____

CHAPTER _____

Student's Name _____ I.D. Number _____

Course _____ Teacher _____ Date _____

1 (A) (B) (C) (D)   11 (A) (B) (C) (D)

2 (A) (B) (C) (D)   12 (A) (B) (C) (D)

3 (A) (B) (C) (D)   13 (A) (B) (C) (D)

4 (A) (B) (C) (D)   14 (A) (B) (C) (D)

5 (A) (B) (C) (D)   15 (A) (B) (C) (D)

6 (A) (B) (C) (D)   16 (A) (B) (C) (D)

7 (A) (B) (C) (D)   17 (A) (B) (C) (D)

8 (A) (B) (C) (D)   18 (A) (B) (C) (D)

9 (A) (B) (C) (D)   19 (A) (B) (C) (D)

10 (A) (B) (C) (D)   20 (A) (B) (C) (D)

21 _____

22 _____

23 _____

24 _____

25 _____

SIDE BY SIDE
Mid-Book & Final Test Answer Sheet

BOOK _____

Check One:
- ☐ MID-BOOK TEST
- ☐ FINAL TEST

Student's Name _____ I.D. Number _____

Course _____ Teacher _____ Date _____

1 Ⓐ Ⓑ Ⓒ Ⓓ   11 Ⓐ Ⓑ Ⓒ Ⓓ   21 Ⓐ Ⓑ Ⓒ Ⓓ   31 Ⓐ Ⓑ Ⓒ Ⓓ
2 Ⓐ Ⓑ Ⓒ Ⓓ   12 Ⓐ Ⓑ Ⓒ Ⓓ   22 Ⓐ Ⓑ Ⓒ Ⓓ   32 Ⓐ Ⓑ Ⓒ Ⓓ
3 Ⓐ Ⓑ Ⓒ Ⓓ   13 Ⓐ Ⓑ Ⓒ Ⓓ   23 Ⓐ Ⓑ Ⓒ Ⓓ   33 Ⓐ Ⓑ Ⓒ Ⓓ
4 Ⓐ Ⓑ Ⓒ Ⓓ   14 Ⓐ Ⓑ Ⓒ Ⓓ   24 Ⓐ Ⓑ Ⓒ Ⓓ   34 Ⓐ Ⓑ Ⓒ Ⓓ
5 Ⓐ Ⓑ Ⓒ Ⓓ   15 Ⓐ Ⓑ Ⓒ Ⓓ   25 Ⓐ Ⓑ Ⓒ Ⓓ   35 Ⓐ Ⓑ Ⓒ Ⓓ
6 Ⓐ Ⓑ Ⓒ Ⓓ   16 Ⓐ Ⓑ Ⓒ Ⓓ   26 Ⓐ Ⓑ Ⓒ Ⓓ   36 Ⓐ Ⓑ Ⓒ Ⓓ
7 Ⓐ Ⓑ Ⓒ Ⓓ   17 Ⓐ Ⓑ Ⓒ Ⓓ   27 Ⓐ Ⓑ Ⓒ Ⓓ   37 Ⓐ Ⓑ Ⓒ Ⓓ
8 Ⓐ Ⓑ Ⓒ Ⓓ   18 Ⓐ Ⓑ Ⓒ Ⓓ   28 Ⓐ Ⓑ Ⓒ Ⓓ   38 Ⓐ Ⓑ Ⓒ Ⓓ
9 Ⓐ Ⓑ Ⓒ Ⓓ   19 Ⓐ Ⓑ Ⓒ Ⓓ   29 Ⓐ Ⓑ Ⓒ Ⓓ   39 Ⓐ Ⓑ Ⓒ Ⓓ
10 Ⓐ Ⓑ Ⓒ Ⓓ   20 Ⓐ Ⓑ Ⓒ Ⓓ   30 Ⓐ Ⓑ Ⓒ Ⓓ   40 Ⓐ Ⓑ Ⓒ Ⓓ

41 _____

42 _____

43 _____

44 _____

45 _____

46 _____

47 _____

48 _____

49 _____

50 _____

Duplication for classroom use is permitted.